TUNDRAS
Frosty, Treeless Lands

BY
LAURA PURDIE SALAS

ILLUSTRATED BY
JEFF YESH

PICTURE WINDOW BOOKS
Minneapolis, Minnesota

Thanks to our advisers for their expertise, research, and advice:

Kim Peterson, Ph.D., Associate Dean, Arts and Sciences
and Professor of Biology
University of Alaska, Anchorage

Terry Flaherty, Ph.D., Professor of English
Minnesota State University, Mankato

Editor: Shelly Lyons
Designer: Lori Bye
Page Production: Melissa Kes
Art Director: Nathan Gassman
Editorial Director: Nick Healy

The illustrations in this book were created digitally.

Picture Window Books
151 Good Counsel Drive
P.O. Box 669
Mankato, MN 56002-0669
877-845-8392
www.picturewindowbooks.com

Photo Credits: Minden Pictures/Michio Hoshino, 23

All books published by Picture Window Books
are manufactured with paper containing at least
10 percent post-consumer waste.

Library of Congress Cataloging-in-Publication Data
Salas, Laura Purdie.
Tundras : frosty, treeless lands / by Laura Purdie Salas ; illustrated by Jeff Yesh.
p. cm. — (Amazing science. Ecosystems)
ISBN 978-1-4048-5376-8 (library binding)
1. Tundra ecology—Juvenile literature. 2. Tundras—Juvenile literature.
I. Yesh, Jeff, 1971- ill. II. Title.
QH541.5.T8S25 2009
577.5'86—dc22
2008037900

Table of Contents

Wide Open Spaces

Look around! Flat, open land surrounds you. Cold, howling wind blows over moss, rocks, and snowy patches. Soggy ground squishes beneath your feet. Caribou gather in the sunlight.

This is the tundra ecosystem. An ecosystem is all of the living and nonliving things in a certain area. It includes plants, animals, water, soil, weather … everything!

FUN FACT
Tundra covers almost 20 percent of Earth's total land surface.

Arctic and Alpine

There are two kinds of tundras: Arctic tundra and alpine tundra.

Arctic tundra is found near the North Pole. Most Arctic tundra is in northern North America, northern Europe, and northern Asia.

Arctic tundra

Alpine tundra is found on mountainsides. Central America, South America, Africa, North America, and Europe all have some alpine tundra.

alpine tundra

FUN FACT

Tundra begins where the forest stops. Trees are not able to grow past the tree line.

Cold and Dry

The Arctic tundra's average winter temperature is minus 30 degrees Fahrenheit (minus 34 degrees Celsius)!

During summer, temperatures rise high enough for the upper layer of ground to thaw. The freezing and thawing of the top layer of soil forces mounds of soil upward. These mounds form patterns called Arctic polygons.

Arctic polygon

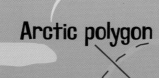

FUN FACT

Tundras are sometimes called Arctic deserts. They receive very little rain or snow. In fact, tundras usually receive only 4 to 10 inches (10 to 25 centimeters) of rain and snow per year.

Small hills called pingos are filled with ice. They form from the pressure caused by freezing water.

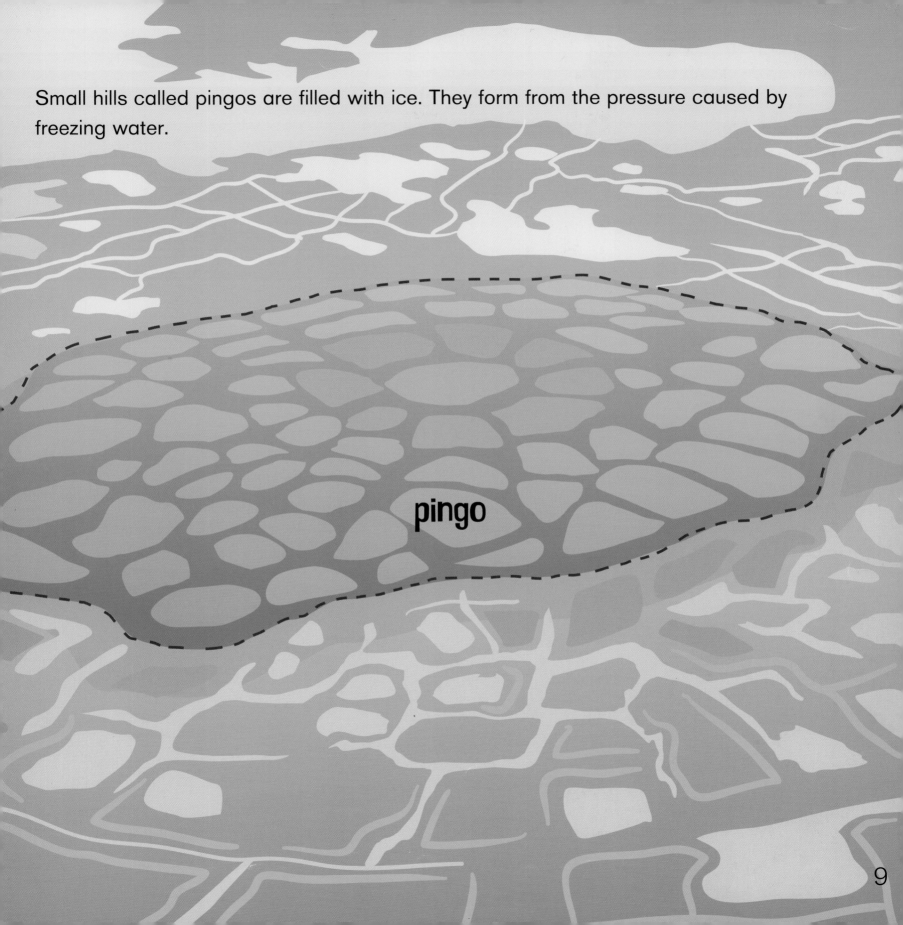

pingo

Animals: Here to Stay

Because of the extreme cold, few animals can live on the Arctic tundra year-round. But some animals make their homes there. These animals include Arctic wolves, musk oxen, brown bears, Arctic hares, and Arctic foxes.

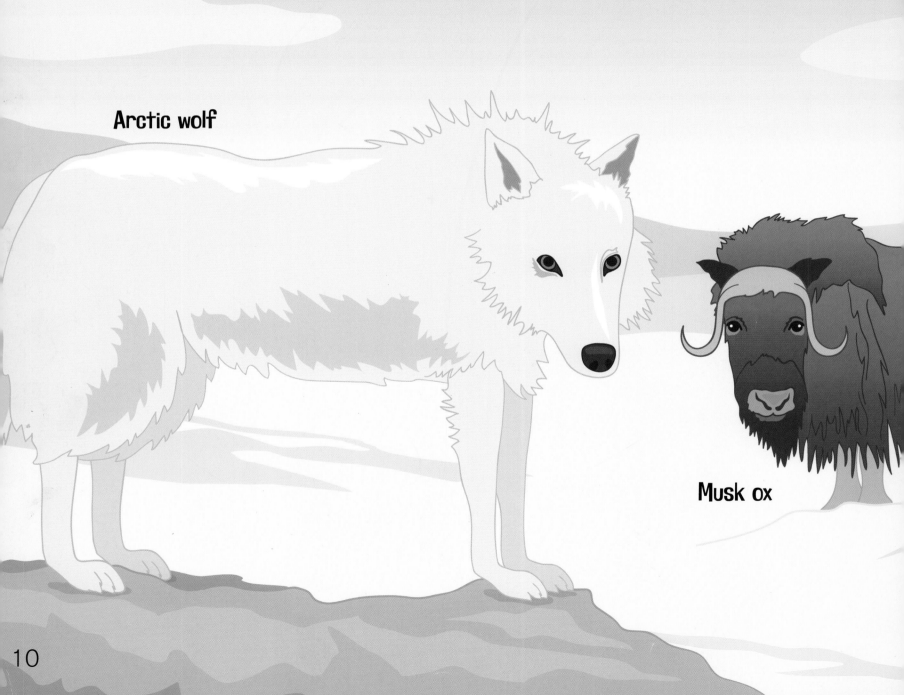

Arctic wolf

Musk ox

Also, some insects, such as mosquitoes, live on the tundra. Mosquito larvae have special chemicals in their blood. The chemicals keep the larvae from freezing during winter.

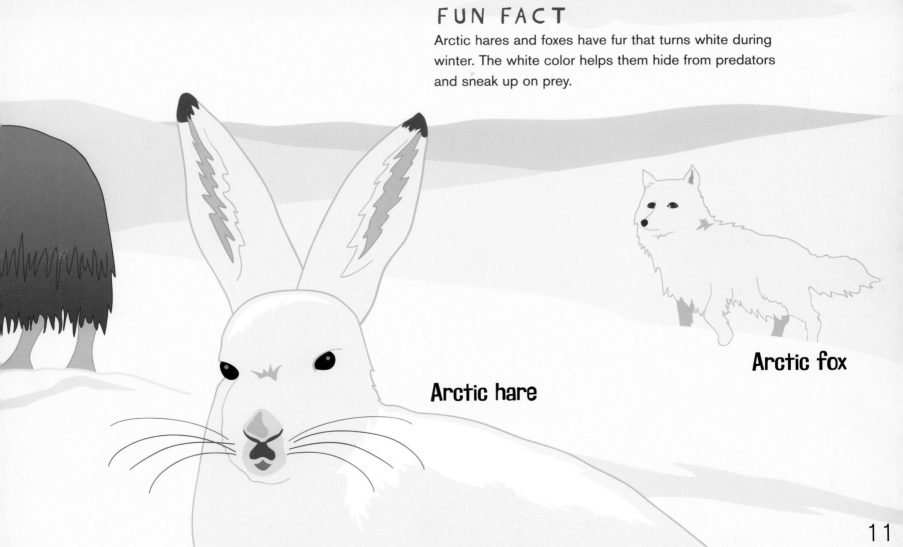

FUN FACT

Arctic hares and foxes have fur that turns white during winter. The white color helps them hide from predators and sneak up on prey.

Arctic fox

Arctic hare

Animals: Just Visiting

Not many animals can survive the long, harsh winters of the tundra. Some just migrate there for the summer. They come for food, to give birth, or for cooler weather. Snow geese, swans, and ducks migrate to the tundra every summer.

Caribou also come. Each spring, thousands of Alaskan caribou walk hundreds of miles over mountains to get to the tundra. Each autumn, they head south again.

FUN FACT

Caribou face dangers during their migration. There is not much food. Wolves and bears hunt them. But the most bothersome hunter of the caribou is the mosquito. Thousands of mosquitoes can swarm a single caribou at one time!

Plants: Low and Protected

The Arctic tundra has long, harsh winters and mostly frozen soil. Still, grasses, mosses, cranberries, and other plants grow there. They stay low to the ground and have short roots. These features help plants survive winters.

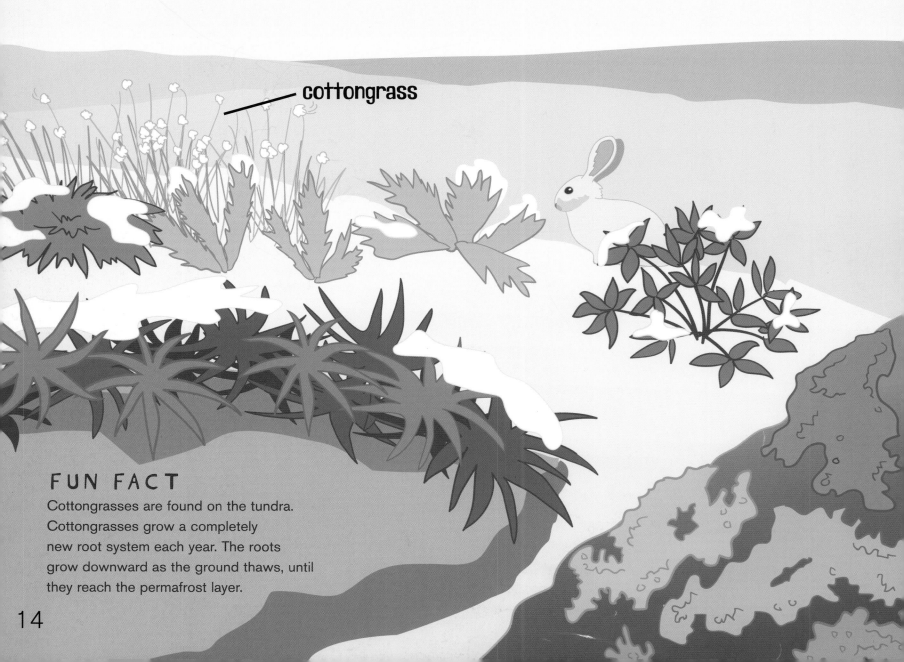

cottongrass

FUN FACT

Cottongrasses are found on the tundra. Cottongrasses grow a completely new root system each year. The roots grow downward as the ground thaws, until they reach the permafrost layer.

When the snow melts in summer, the ground doesn't totally thaw. A layer below the surface, called permafrost, stays frozen all year. In some areas, ice wedges form in the soil. This frozen soil can't absorb melted snow, so the tundra turns soggy each spring. The thawing of the top layer of soil allows some plants to grow during summer months.

ice wedge

Alpine Tundra

Alpine tundra has some things in common with Arctic tundra. At times, both areas get very cold. Also, many alpine tundra plants are the same as those found on Arctic tundra.

But Alpine tundra has differences, too. Alpine tundra animals include mountain sheep, mountain goats, birds, squirrels, and pikas.

mountain sheep

FUN FACT

Many plants on the alpine tundra grow near the ground. There they can avoid the wind. They may also be dark in color, so they can take in the sun's heat. Grasses are also found there.

16

Alpine tundra can also be warmer than Arctic tundra. Alpine tundras located in tropical climates have cold nights and warm to hot days all year long.

mountain goat

pika

white-tailed ptarmigan

ground squirrel

Why We Need Tundras

Tundra is important to our planet. Plants and animals make their homes there. The Arctic tundra also holds useful natural resources such as oil, copper, and coal.

Farmers use alpine tundra lands for grazing cattle and growing crops. People who live on the tundra need its resources for survival. They fish, hunt, gather eggs, and pick berries on the tundra.

FUN FACT

The Sámi people of Norway and Sweden have herded reindeer for centuries. They used to be nomads, following herds across the tundra. Today, reindeer herders use snowmobiles and other tools in their work. Some Sámi high school students even study reindeer herding at school!

Harsh and Fragile

Tundra looks tough, but it is fragile. Air pollution from all over the world gathers in a haze above the Arctic tundra. The pollution traps the sun's heat in Earth's atmosphere. The heat makes temperatures milder. A change in the temperatures means a change in the balance of life on the Arctic tundra.

FUN FACT
Drilling for oil in the tundra can cause pollution of the area's air, ground, and water.

Sometimes, people destroy alpine tundra grazing lands to build ski slopes. Then they build roads, hotels, and restaurants for the tourists.

Both kinds of tundra play important roles in our world. The tundra has many gifts for us, but we must be careful not to destroy it.

Tundra Diorama: Tundra in a Box

What You Need:

- a shoebox
- light blue and light green paint
- a paintbrush
- potpourri
- sandpaper
- glue
- blue or gray construction paper
- small twigs
- pictures of spring tundra animals, such as caribou, foxes, and polar bears

What You Do:

1. Turn the shoebox on its side.
2. Paint the sides and the top blue.
3. Cut sandpaper to fit the bottom, and paint most of it green. Leave some brown patches.
4. Glue construction paper "puddles" to your sandpaper, and glue them inside the box.
5. Glue down twigs to look like shrubs.
6. Glue pictures of spring tundra animals in your diorama. Glue small groups of potpourri on the "ground" and lower sides to add some spring flowers.

Tundra Facts

Arctic tundra

- The Northern Lights sometimes ripple and wave in the tundra sky. Flares from the sun send energy toward Earth. When that energy hits Earth's sky, it creates beautiful lights. Northern Lights might be red, green, purple, and blue.

- In December and January, the sun does not rise on the Arctic tundra. It is dark nearly all of the time.

- The layer of permafrost on the Arctic tundra in Alaska varies in thickness. In some areas, it is only about 12 inches (30 cm) thick. But in some areas, the permafrost stretches more than 2,000 feet (610 m) below the surface!

Glossary

Arctic polygons—features such as circles, squares, or hexagons on the soil surface; caused by repeated freezing and thawing of the soil

ecosystem—an area with certain animals, plants, weather, and land or water features

larvae—wingless young insects

migrate—to regularly move from place to place to find food, shelter, or a mate

nomads—people who move from place to place and have no permanent home

permafrost—a layer of frozen earth underground that never thaws, even in summer

pingos—ice-cored mounds found in permafrost lands; caused by freezing

predators—animals that hunt and eat other animals

prey—an animal that is hunted and eaten for food

soil—another word for dirt

tree line—a boundary past which trees cannot grow

tropical climates—warm places near Earth's equator

tundra—an ecosystem known for its extremely low temperatures, lack of trees, and land that is shaped by the freezing and thawing of the soil

To Learn More

More Books to Read

Fleisher, Paul. *Tundra Food Webs.* Minneapolis: Lerner, 2008.

Frisch, Aaron. *Tundra.* Mankato, Minn.: Creative Education, 2008.

McKissack, Fredrick Jr., and Lisa Beringer McKissack. *Counting in the Tundra.* Berkeley Heights, N.J.: Enslow Elementary, 2008.

On the Web

FactHound offers a safe, fun way to find educator-approved Internet sites related to this book.

Here's what you do:
1. Visit *www.facthound.com*
2. Choose your grade level.
3. Begin your search.

This book's ID number is 9781404853768

Index

Look for all of the books in the Amazing Science—Ecosystems series: